EARLY SKILLS LIBRARY

songs & poems

Developed by Macmillan Educational Company
Written by Marilyn LaPenta
Text illustrated by John O'Brien
Cover illustrated by Patrick Girouard

Newbridge Educational Programs

TABLE OF CONTENTS

SECTION ONE—GETTING-ACQUAINTED SONGS

Grade Level

N–K	THE GREEN DRESS	5
	Classroom Song	
N–1	SING A SONG OF GREETING	6
	Song / Circle Game	
N–2	WHAT IS YOUR NAME?	7–8
	Classroom Chant / Name-Tag Patterns	
N–2	BIRTHDAYS, TELEPHONE NUMBERS, AND ADDRESSES	9
	Chants for Everyone	
K–2	PAWPAW PATCH	10
	Song / Skipping Game	

SECTION TWO—DRAMATIZATION SONGS AND ACTIVITIES

N–K	MISS POLLY	11
	Action Song	
N–1	ROBOT, ROBOT, MARCH AROUND	12
	Action Song	
N–1	AINSI FONT	13–14
	Traditional French Song / Hand Motions / Clown Marionette Teaching Aid	
N–2	WAKE ME! SHAKE ME!	15–16
	Song / Actions / Sequencing Worksheet	
K–2	RIG-A-JIG-JIG	17
	English Folk Song / Circle Game	

SECTION THREE—MOVEMENT ACTIVITIES

Grade Level

N–1	JIM ALONG JOSIE	18
	American Folk Song / Circle Game	
N–1	ROLL THAT RED BALL	19
	Action Song / Ball Game	
N–1	BLUEBIRD, BLUEBIRD	20
	Song / Skipping Game	
N–2	RATTLE AND SHAKE!	21
	Handmade Percussion Instruments	
K–1	RHYTHMS 'N' RHYMES	22
	Action Poems	
K–2	OLD BRASS WAGON	23
	Song / Circle Game	
1–2	BOUNCE THAT BALL!	24
	Nonsense Rhymes / Action Games	
1–2	JAZZY JINGLES	25–26
	Playground Chants	

SECTION FOUR—LISTENING AND RHYMING SONGS

N–1	ANIMAL ECHOES	27
	Rhyming Story / Body Movements	
N–1	UP THE SCALE AND DOWN	28
	Musical Scales	
N–2	A-HUNTING WE WILL GO	29
	Rhyming Song / Art Activity	

TABLE OF CONTENTS
Continued

Grade Level

N–2 JOHN JACOB JINGLEHEIMER SCHMIDT 30
      Loud and Soft Sounds
N–2 A RAM-SAM-SAM 31
      Moroccan Song / Hand Motions
N–2 BINGO AND VARIATIONS 32
      Clapping Song
K–2 BILL GROGAN'S GOAT 33–34
      Echo Song / Worksheet
K–2 DOWN BY THE BAY 35
      Rhyming Song

SECTION FIVE—CONCEPT SONGS: Body Awareness

N–1 OPEN, SHUT THEM 36
      Song / Hand Motions
N–1 WIGGLY SONG 37
      Action Song
N–2 AIKEN DRUM 38
      Silly Song
N–2 IF YOU'RE HAPPY AND YOU KNOW IT 39
      Action Song
K–2 DO YOUR EARS HANG LOW? 40
      Silly Song / Hand Motions

SECTION SIX —CONCEPT SONGS: Numbers and Counting

N–1 ONE IN THE BED 41–42
      Counting Song / Art Activity / Visual Aid
N–2 THIS OLD MAN 43–45
      Counting Song / Hand and Body Motions / Rhyming
      Worksheets
N–2 JOHNNY WORKS WITH ONE HAMMER 46
      Counting Song / Hand and Body Motions

Grade Level

N–2 THE ANTS GO MARCHING 47–49
      Action Song / Counting Worksheets

SECTION SEVEN—SILLY SONGS AND POEMS

N–2 NOBODY LIKES ME 50
      Song / Discussion Questions
N–2 A PEANUT SAT ON A RAILROAD TRACK 51–52
      Song / Peanut-Butter Recipe / Art Activity /
      Animal Cutouts
1–2 TRICKY TONGUE TWISTERS 53
      Make a Minibook
1–2 INSIDE OUT AND UPSIDE DOWN 54
      Nonsense Rhymes / Poem Starters
1–2 NEVER ENOUGH NONSENSE 55
      Worksheet

SECTION EIGHT—HOLIDAY SONGS

N–1 THE GOBLIN IN THE DARK 56
      Halloween Song
N–2 FIVE FAT TURKEYS AND VARIATIONS 57–58
      Thanksgiving Song / Finger Plays
N–2 WE WISH YOU A MERRY CHRISTMAS AND VARIATIONS . . 59
      Christmas Song / Movement Activity
N–2 THE ANGEL BAND 60
      Christmas Song / Rhythm Activity
N–1 TONY CHESTNUT 61
      Valentine's Day Song / Hand Motions
N–1 HOP OVER, BUNNY 62
      Easter Song / Bunny-Ears Headband
N–2 MICHAEL FINNEGAN 63–64
      St. Patrick's Day Song / Worksheet

THE GREEN DRESS
Classroom Song

When - ev - er *(child's name)* has a   green dress on,   green dress on,   green dress on, When -

ev - er *(child's name)* has a   green dress   on,   we will sing a song   for   her.

Steps:

1. Sing this song with your class at the beginning of the year to help children learn one another's names. Form a circle with your class and teach children the song, following the steps below.

2. Choose one child to stand in the center of the circle.

3. Sing the song above, substituting words describing something special that the child in the center of the circle is wearing.

   Whenever Johnny has his blue shirt on . . .
   Whenever Tommy has his new shoes on . . .
   Whenever Mary has braids in her hair . . .
   Whenever Marissa has her sweat suit on . . .

4. Give each child a turn to stand in the center of the circle as you sing something special about him or her. Once the children are familiar with the song, let the child choose the special feature about himself or herself.

Variation:

Make this a color song. Sing about a particular color one day. Tell the class: "Let's first sing about each of the children who are wearing green today." Then sing verses about those children and whatever they have on that is that color.

SING A SONG OF GREETING
Song / Circle Game

Use this activity to help children get acquainted with one another or to introduce newcomers to the class.

Steps:

1. Ask children to stand in a large circle.

2. Choose one child to stand in the center of the circle.

3. Sing the following words to the tune of "Frère Jacques."

All sing:	*Where is* (name of child in center)? *Where is* (name of child in center)?
Child in center:	*Here I am. Here I am.*
All:	*How are you today, Sir* (or *Miss*)?
Child in center:	*Very well I thank you.*
All:	*Glad you're here.* *Glad you're here.*

4. At the end of the verse, the child in the center of the circle will tap another child, who will then step into the center while the first child returns to the circle.

5. Repeat the song until each child has had a turn standing in the center.

Variation:

Have each child draw a large picture of himself or herself. To the same tune, have the children sing:

I am special. I am special.
Look at me. Look at me.
Ask me why I'm special. I'll be glad to tell you.
Yes, I will. Yes, I will.

Then ask the children, one at a time, to hold up their pictures and tell something about themselves—what they most like to do or play, what their favorite food, color, or song is, and so on.

Use this tune or any similar sing-song chant to help children
learn the names of their classmates.

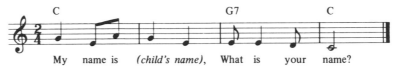

My name is (child's name), What is your name?

3. Clap the rhythm of a child's name and see whether that child can identify his or her name. Use first and last names. Several children may have names with the same rhythm. Have each child whisper his or her name into both hands and then clap out a rhythm for that name. Use this activity when children are lining up or to regain their attention before starting an activity.

Steps:

1. Ask children to sit cross-legged in a circle.

2. Sing the tune above, filling in your name. Point to a child, or look at the child next to you, and have that child sing the chant, filling in his or her name. That child then points to another child, or looks at the child next to him or her, who will repeat the tune.

3. Continue singing the chant until all the children have identified themselves.

Variations:

1. Another day, after the above chant has been introduced, add a variation. Each child must say his or her name and give the name of something that begins with the same sound as his or her name. For example: "My name is Joan and I like jam." Older children may also name a place that begins with the same sound, e.g., "My name is Marilyn, I come from Maryland, and I like meatballs."

2. Chant the verse without music, filling in your name and beating a drum to each beat. Pass the drum to the next person in the circle, and have him or her beat out the rhythm to his or her name.

Suggestion:

Reproduce the name-tag patterns on page 8 several times. Let each child choose an animal and write his or her name on it with a dark marker. Have children lightly color the animals and cut them out. Punch a hole in each animal and tie a long piece of yarn through it to make a necklace. Children may wear their name tags during these games.

BIRTHDAYS, TELEPHONE NUMBERS, AND ADDRESSES
Chants for Everyone

Use these simple chants at the beginning of the year to familiarize children with their birthdays, telephone numbers, and addresses.

Steps:

1. Have the class stand in a large circle.

2. Choose one child to stand in the center of the circle.

3. Ask children to recite a chant as the child in the center closes his or her eyes and turns around slowly, pointing one finger straight out toward the circle. The rest of the class claps on the beat.

4. On the last word of the chant, the child to whom the child in the center is pointing must name his or her birthday (or address or phone number, depending on the chant). After responding, he or she takes the place of the child in the center of the circle. If the child does not answer correctly, tell him or her the answer and ask the child to stay in place until he or she can give the correct response next time. The child in the center remains there for another turn.

Variations:

1. Choose a child to walk around the outside of the circle, lightly tapping a child on the shoulder on each beat of the chant. The child who is tapped on the last word of the chant has to name his or her birthday (or telephone number or address). That child then replaces the first child and walks around the circle tapping others.

2. Have children sit in a circle and pass around a ball, potato, or similar object as they say a chant. The object is passed around to the beat. The child who has the object on the last word names his or her birthday and sits in the middle of the circle. Play the game until all children but one are sitting in the middle. The last child receives a special privilege that day (first to line up for lunch or recess, and so on).

BIRTHDAY CHANT
Apples, pears, peaches, plums,
Tell me when your birthday comes.

TELEPHONE-NUMBER CHANT
Cake, candy, ice-cream cone,
Tell me the number of your telephone.

ADDRESS CHANT
Rabbit, cat, squirrel, mouse,
Tell me the number on your house.

PAWPAW PATCH
Song / Skipping Game

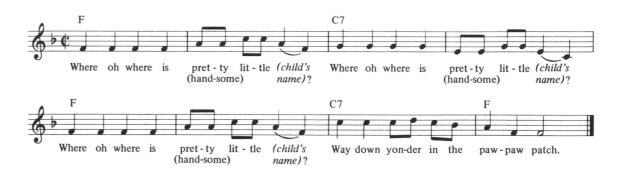

Where oh where is pret-ty lit-tle *(child's* (hand-some) *name)?* Where oh where is pret-ty lit-tle *(child's* (hand-some) *name)?*

Where oh where is pret-ty lit-tle *(child's* (hand-some) *name)?* Way down yon-der in the paw-paw patch.

Verse 2

Picking up pawpaws, put them in the basket,
(repeat two times)
Way down yonder in the pawpaw patch.

Verse 3

Picking up pawpaws, put them in your pocket,
(repeat two times)
Way down yonder in the pawpaw patch.

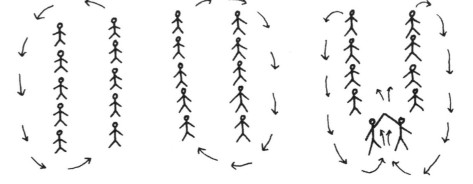

Verse 1   Verse 2   Verse 3

Steps:

1. Teach children the song on this page. Then divide your class into two single files, with the children facing forward. The two lines should stand parallel and about 3′ apart.

2. All children sing the first verse, filling in the name of the first child in the left-hand line. While they sing, the first child in the right-hand line will lead his or her line in skipping counterclockwise once around the line on the left. As they skip, the children will shade their eyes with their hands as if looking for someone. The children in the left-hand line stand in place, clapping in time to the music.

3. When the second verse is sung, the children in the left-hand line will skip clockwise once around the other line, bending down as if they are picking up fruits and putting them in baskets. The children in the right-hand line stand in place and clap to the beat.

4. On the third verse, children in each line will skip, circling to the outside away from the other line. The children should pantomime picking up pawpaws and putting them in their pockets as they skip. When the leaders of the two lines meet, they join hands and raise them to form an arch. The other children pass under the arch, staying in their lines. The two children forming the arch then join the ends of their respective lines.

5. Repeat the song several times to give each child a turn to be a leader, or for as long as it holds children's interest.

Note: The pawpaw is a bananalike fruit that grows on a tree. The pawpaw tree grows primarily in the southern United States.

MISS POLLY
Action Song

Miss Pol - ly had a dol - ly who was sick, sick, sick, So she
called for the doc-tor to be quick, quick, quick. The doc - tor came_ with his
bag and his hat, And he knocked at the door_ with a rat - tat - tat.

You need: doll
two play telephones
doctor's bag
hat
wood blocks
doll bed or box

Steps:

1. Teach children the song and actions on this page.

2. Assign one child to be Miss Polly (or Mr. Wally), and another to be the doctor. Make sure to let boys and girls have turns playing both roles. When necessary, change the pronouns in the song depending on whether boys or girls are playing the roles.

3. Let pairs of children act out the song as it is sung, using the props listed above.

4. If desired, omit using the props. Divide the class into pairs of children and assign the roles of the doctor and Miss Polly or Mr. Wally to the children in each pair. Let all the pairs of children sing and act out the song together.

Miss Polly had a dolly who was sick, sick, sick.	(Polly shakes head and looks at doll.)
So she called for the doctor to be quick, quick, quick,	(Polly dials one telephone and doctor answers the other one.)
The doctor came with his bag and his hat,	(Doctor approaches wearing hat and carrying bag.)
And he knocked at the door with a rat-tat-tat.	(Doctor pretends to knock on door; another child may clap wood blocks three times.)
And he looked at the dolly, and he shook his head,	(Doctor looks at doll and shakes head.)
And he said, "Miss Polly, put her straight to bed.	(Doctor shakes finger at Polly.)
She soon will be rid of her chill, chill, chill,	(Polly puts doll in bed.)
And I'll see you in the morning with my bill, bill, bill."	(Doctor stands with right hand extended, palm up.)

ROBOT, ROBOT, MARCH AROUND
Action Song

Teach children the song on this page and have them act out the different verses.

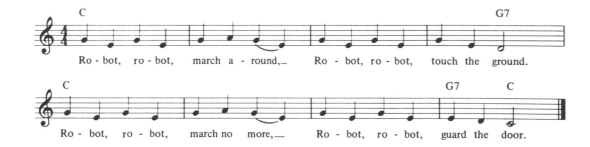

Ro - bot, ro - bot, march a - round,— Ro - bot, ro - bot, touch the ground.

Ro - bot, ro - bot, march no more,— Ro - bot, ro - bot, guard the door.

Verse 1

Robot, robot, march around.	(March around like a robot.)
Robot, robot, touch the ground.	(Bend stiffly to touch the ground.)
Robot, robot, march no more.	(Stand still and straight.)
Robot, robot, guard the door.	(Hold arms out to sides.)

Verse 2

Robot, robot, oil your machine.	(Pat chest with both hands.)
Robot, robot, wipe it clean.	(Brush hands together in wiping motion.)
Robot, robot, now sit down.	(Sit down in seat or on floor.)
Robot, robot, ride to town.	(Pretend to drive robot vehicle.)

Verse 3

Robot, robot, do not roam.	(March in small circles.)
Robot, robot, march back home.	(March back to seat.)
Robot, robot, shut your light.	(Twist nose with fingers.)
Robot, robot, say "Good night."	(Put hands together and lean head to the side, resting it on hands.)

Variations:

1. Encourage children to add their own verses, imagining what they would like a robot to do for them, e.g., "Tie my shoe . . . that will do," "Pull my sled . . . make my bed."

2. Make up verses using other characters, such as monster, soldier, and monkey.

3. Sing the song, using a child's name. The child named must do the actions mentioned in the song. Sing additional verses, naming another child and different actions each time.

Ain-si font, font, font, Les pe-ti-tes ma-rion-net-tes. Ain-si font, font, font, Trois petits tours Et puis s'en vont.

Verse 1

Ainsi font, font, font,
Les petites marionnettes.   (Children twist their hands back and forth, holding them in front.)
Ainsi font, font, font,
Trois petits tours   (Children rotate their hands over each other three times.)
Et puis s'en vont.   (Children hide hands behind their backs.)

Verse 2

See them go, just so,   (Repeat actions for verse 1.)
The little marionettes.
See them go, just so,
Three little turns
And away they go.

You need: a piano
the assistance of your school music teacher

Steps:

1. Before teaching this song to the class, make the marionette described on page 14 and show children how it moves. Or bring in a real marionette to show children.

2. Have the music teacher play this song on the piano for the class. Then teach the children the French verse, letting them repeat each line after you. Teach the hand motions as you sing the song.

3. Teach the children the translation, explaining that this is what the song means.

4. Ask the children to pretend to be marionettes. Have them move their arms and legs in marionette fashion and turn around three times as they sing along with the recording, while you move the marionette in time to the music.

Follow-up Activity:

Let one child move the marionette as the other children sing the song and pantomime the actions of a marionette. Repeat the song, giving each child a turn to manipulate the marionette. Continue for as long as interest lasts.

You need: colored construction paper
toilet paper tube
transparent tape
scissors
3″ oaktag circle
glue
buttons
yarn scraps
ruler
1 yard of heavy, thick yarn or cord
masking tape
colored felt
two plastic-foam egg-carton cups
medium-weight yarn
two thin 10″ to 12″ sticks or dowels
needle and strong white thread

Steps:

1. Wrap colored construction paper around the toilet paper tube, tape in place, and trim to fit. This is the clown's body.

2. Use the oaktag circle to make the clown's head. Glue on two buttons for eyes. Make hair, a nose, and a mouth by gluing on different colored yarn scraps.

3. With scissors, poke a hole in the toilet paper tube ½″ from one open end.

4. Thread a 12″ piece of thick yarn or cord through the hole, knotting one end inside the tube. (For easier threading, wrap a piece of tape around the ends of the yarn or cord.) This forms the clown's neck.

5. Use masking tape to attach the free end of the neck to the back of the clown's head.

6. To make the arms, cut a 1″ × 10″ strip of colored felt. Trim the short ends of the strip to look like hands. Glue the center of the strip on the center of the body just below the neck so that the arms dangle loosely.

7. Near the other end of the toilet paper tube, poke two holes on either side. These holes should be near the underside of the tube, with the hole for the neck being on the top side of the tube.

8. Thread a 12″ piece of cord or yarn through each hole and knot it inside the tube. These are the clown's legs.

9. To make the feet, place the plastic-foam egg-carton cups with the open ends down. Poke a hole in the center of the round area of each egg carton cup. Thread the free end of a piece of "leg" yarn through an egg carton cup and knot it inside the cup. Repeat with the other egg carton cup.

10. Next, use medium-weight yarn to tie the two sticks or dowels in an **X** shape, as shown. Thread a needle with a 16″ piece of strong white thread and knot the end. Sew up through the clown's body, just behind the neck, and tie the thread securely to one end of one stick or dowel.

11. Knot and sew another long piece of thread through the top center of the clown's head. With one hand, hold up the sticks or dowels with the body attached. Wind the free end of the thread around the opposite end of the same stick attached to the body, so that the head and body hang evenly. Tie the thread securely in place.

12. Knot and sew a long piece of thread through the top of each foot. Hold the marionette up so that the feet just touch the floor as you wind each piece of thread around opposite ends of the free stick or dowel. Tie the threads so they are taut.

13. Use this marionette as a teaching aid when singing "Ainsi Font" on page 13, and let children experiment with manipulating it.

Verse 1

Wake me! (clap clap) *Shake me!* (clap clap)
Don't let me sleep too long! (clap clap)
Got to get up so early in the mornin',
And sing you this happy song.

Suggested Variations for Line 3

Got to stretch my arms so early in the mornin',
Got to comb my hair so early in the mornin',
Got to brush my teeth so early in the mornin',
Got to dress myself so early in the mornin',
Got to eat my breakfast so early in the mornin',
Got to run to the bus stop so early In
in the mornin',

Steps:

1. This song may be used to initiate a discussion and activities on proper eating and sleeping habits. Teach children the first verse. Have children clap their hands as indicated. If desired, let one or two children beat a tambourine or other rhythm instrument on these notes.

2. Let children talk about what they do in the morning after waking up. Then sing the song again, substituting one of the suggested lines for the third line of the song. Have children dramatize the various morning activities mentioned as they sing. Repeat the song several times. Add the lines suggested and any others the children might invent.

Follow-up Activity:

Use the worksheet on page 16 as a follow-up sequencing activity.

Look at the four pictures at the bottom of the page. Color them and cut them out. In the numbered boxes, paste the pictures in order. Begin with the picture that shows what you do first in the morning and end with the picture that shows what you do last.

Name_____

1

2

3

4

Then I get dressed.

First I wake up.

Now I'm ready to go to school!

Next I eat a good breakfast.

As I was walk-ing down the street, down the street, down the street, My good friend I

chanced to meet, hi-ho, hi-ho,— hi-ho.— Rig-a-jig-jig and a-way we go, a-

way we go, a-way we go. Rig-a-jig-jig and a-way we go, hi-ho, hi-ho,— hi-ho!—

Verse

As I was walking down the street, down the street, down the street,
My good friend I chanced to meet, hi-ho, hi-ho, hi-ho.

Chorus

Rig-a-jig-jig and away we go, away we go, away we go.
Rig-a-jig-jig and away we go, hi-ho, hi-ho, hi-ho!

Steps:

1. Ask children to stand in a large circle and teach them the song.

2. Choose a boy and a girl (or any two children) to stand outside the circle.

3. As the song is sung, the two children standing outside the circle walk clockwise around the circle, each looking for a friend. By the time the first *hi-ho* is sung, each child should have tapped a friend on the shoulder, signaling him or her to stand outside the circle with that child.

4. On the chorus, everyone sings and claps as the two pairs of children skip hand in hand clockwise around the outside of the circle.

5. At the end of the chorus, the original two children go back into the circle, in their friends' places. The friends now walk around the circle and pick new friends as the song is repeated.

Variation:

Have the class form small circles of six to eight children. Choose one child from each circle to walk around outside the circle and tap a friend on the shoulder. Encourage children to give everyone a turn.

JIM ALONG JOSIE
American Folk Song / Circle Game

Hi!   Come a-long   Jim   a-long   Jo - sie,   Hi!   Come a-long   Jim   a-long   Joe.

Steps:

1. Have the class stand in a circle.

2. Sing the chorus, asking the children to face the center of the circle and clap their hands to the music. Repeat the chorus, and have the children sing with you.

3. Tell the children you will now ask them to move around the circle. They must listen carefully so they know what to do.

4. Sing one of the following verses to the tune above while the children move around the circle.

   Hop! Hop along Jim along Josie . . .

   Skip! Skip along . . .

   Hi! Gallop along . . .

   Run! Run along . . .

   Walk! Walk along . . .

   Crawl! Crawl along . . .

   Hi! Tiptoe along . . .

   Slide! Slide along . . .

5. Between verses, ask the children to face the center of the circle and clap hands as they sing the chorus, waiting to hear what they should do next.

Variations:

1. Use this song as a following-directions activity. Some suggested verses are: "Clap your hands," "Snap your fingers," and "Tap your toes." You may also use this song to review the names of body parts—"Tap your head" (nose, ears, and so on).

2. Use this song to teach children to identify and play various instruments. Distribute different rhythm instruments to the class. Sing: "Play the drum, Jim along. . ." As you sing a verse, the child or children holding the instrument named will play it.

3. Use the simple tune for instant classroom management.

   Time to line (clean) up, Jim along Josie,
   Time to line (clean) up, Jim along Joe.
   When I tap you, Jim along Josie,
   Then you line (clean) up, Jim along Joe.

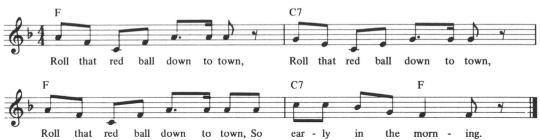

Roll that red ball down to town, Roll that red ball down to town,

Roll that red ball down to town, So ear-ly in the morn-ing.

You need: 8″ rubber ball

Steps:

1. Divide your class into two equal groups. Have the groups form two straight lines, 6′ to 8′ apart. Children in one line should face the children opposite them.

2. Teach the song to the children.

3. Repeat the song, this time having one child at the end of a line roll the ball to the child opposite him or her. That child will roll the ball to the second person in the opposite line as the song is repeated. Children will roll the ball back and forth between the two lines until it reaches the last child.

4. Let the last child begin the action for the next verse. Vary subsequent verses by changing the action—for example, "Bounce that red ball," "Toss that red ball," "Kick that red ball."

Variations:

1. Make pompon balls of yarn or use balls of soft sponge. The balls should be of different colors. Place them all at the head of the line and name a different color in each verse. The first child must choose the correct ball and roll it across to the child opposite.

2. Use more than one ball and teach ordinal numbers with this song. Begin with "Roll that first ball." Continue with "Roll that second ball," and then "Roll that third ball." Children will have to be quick! After they roll one ball they must get ready to catch and roll another one.

BLUEBIRD, BLUEBIRD
Song / Skipping Game

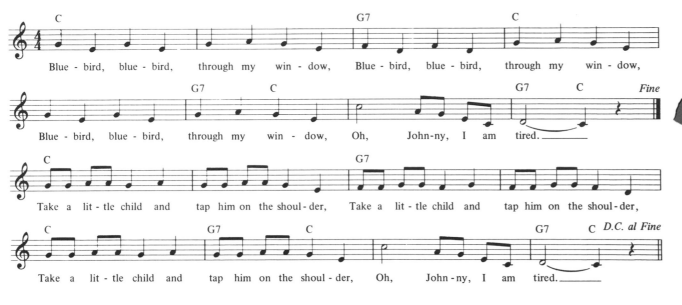

Blue - bird, blue - bird, through my win - dow, Blue - bird, blue - bird, through my win - dow,

Blue - bird, blue - bird, through my win - dow, Oh, John - ny, I am tired. *Fine*

Take a lit - tle child and tap him on the shoul - der, Take a lit - tle child and tap him on the shoul - der,

Take a lit - tle child and tap him on the shoul - der, Oh, John - ny, I am tired. *D.C. al Fine*

Chorus

Bluebird, bluebird, through my window,
Bluebird, bluebird, through my window,
Bluebird, bluebird, through my window,
Oh, Johnny, I am tired.

Verse

Take a little child and tap him on the shoulder,
(repeat two times)
Oh, Johnny, I am tired.

Steps:

1. Have children stand in a large circle and join hands. Teach them the song.

2. Choose one child to be the bluebird and have him or her stand outside the circle.

3. The children in the circle raise their joined hands to form arches as they begin the chorus. All sing the chorus while the bluebird skips in and out of the circle through the arches. On the last word of the chorus, *tired,* the bluebird stops.

4. The bluebird stands behind the child closest to where he or she stopped. The bluebird taps that child lightly on the shoulder as everyone sings the verse. If the bluebird taps a boy on the shoulder, have the class change the word *child* in the verse to *boy.* If the bluebird taps a girl, change the words *boy* and *him* in the verse to *girl* and *her.*

5. Children sing the chorus again, while the new bluebird skips in and out between the arches and the "tired" bluebird takes that child's place in the circle. Repeat the song and game several times to give as many children as possible a turn.

Variation:

After the first bluebird taps a friend, the two of them skip through the arches of the circle. Then they each pick another child so that four bluebirds are weaving through the arches. Each of the four bluebirds picks another child and so on, until all the children are skipping in a circle.

JINGLE BELLS

You need: 1½″ × 6″ pieces of felt or fabric
(one for each child)
heavy yarn, cut into 24″ lengths
large-eye needles
small bells (three for each child)

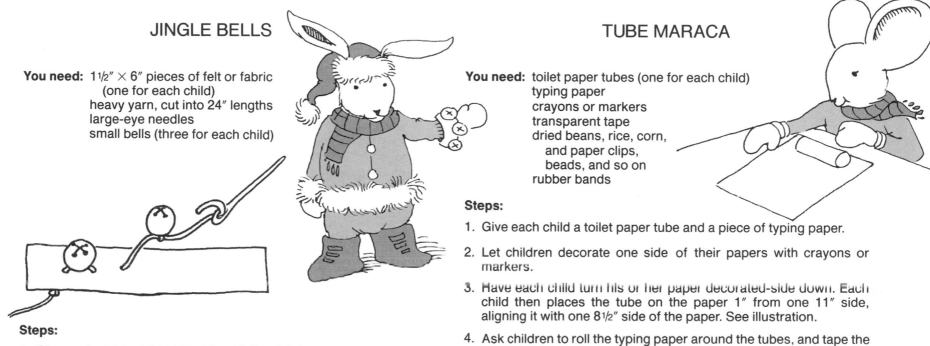

Steps:

1. Give each child a 1½″ × 6″ strip of felt or fabric.

2. Thread 24″ lengths of yarn through the needles. Tie a knot in each yarn piece, leaving about 4″ of yarn below each knot.

3. Instruct each child to begin sewing about 1″ from the end of the fabric strip, pushing the needle up through the felt or fabric.

4. Have each child thread the yarn through the loop on a bell.

5. Each child will then sew down through the felt or fabric, close to where the needle just came through from the other side.

6. Leaving a little space (about 1″), each child will sew up through the fabric again. Have each child attach another bell by following steps 4 and 5.

7. Each child will attach the third bell in the same way.

8. Help children knot the yarn behind the fabric.

9. Children may shake their jingle bells by tying the two ends of the yarn together in bows and slipping the fabric loops over their wrists. They may also clasp the loops in their fists at the yarn ties.

TUBE MARACA

You need: toilet paper tubes (one for each child)
typing paper
crayons or markers
transparent tape
dried beans, rice, corn,
and paper clips,
beads, and so on
rubber bands

Steps:

1. Give each child a toilet paper tube and a piece of typing paper.

2. Let children decorate one side of their papers with crayons or markers.

3. Have each child turn his or her paper decorated-side down. Each child then places the tube on the paper 1″ from one 11″ side, aligning it with one 8½″ side of the paper. See illustration.

4. Ask children to roll the typing paper around the tubes, and tape the paper in place.

5. Next, have each child fold the 1″ overlapping edge over the end of the tube. Tape to seal.

6. Holding the sealed side down, each child will fill the tube with a handful of one of the items listed above (dried beans, rice, corn, and so on). Encourage children to choose fillings that will make interesting sounds.

7. Assist each child with wrapping a rubber band tightly around the open end of the typing paper, close to the tube. This excess paper forms the handle for the maraca.

8. Children shake their maracas to music and listen to the different sounds, experimenting by shaking them gently and hard to make soft and loud sounds. Let one or two children at a time shake their maracas so the others can hear the various sounds.

You need: drum
tambourine
rhythm sticks

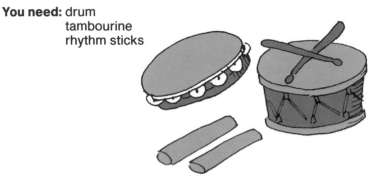

Steps:

1. Recite some of the Mother Goose rhymes on this page.

2. Let your class listen to the beat as you tap out the rhythm for each rhyme on a drum, tambourine, or on rhythm sticks.

3. Then ask children to form a circle and skip (or gallop or march) to the beat.

4. Vary the movement and improve the children's listening skills by assigning an instrument to a particular movement—for example, "Gallop when you hear the rhythm sticks. Walk when you hear the drum. Skip when you hear the tambourine."

THE GRAND OLD DUKE OF YORK
marching poem

The grand old Duke of York,
He had ten thousand men.
He marched them up a very high hill,
And he marched them down again.
And when he was up he was up,
And when he was down he was down;
And when he was only halfway up,
He was neither up nor down.

RIDE AWAY, JOHNNY
galloping poem

Ride away, ride away,
Johnny shall ride,
And he shall have Pussy Cat
Tied to one side.
He shall have Puppy Dog
Tied to the other,
And Johnny shall ride
To see his grandmother.

RIDE A COCK HORSE
galloping poem
(Use handmade bells described on page 21.)

Ride a cock horse
To Banbury Cross,
To see a fair lady upon a white horse;
With rings on her fingers
And bells on her toes,
She shall have music wherever she goes.

TO MARKET
skipping or galloping poem

To market, to market, to buy a fat pig.
Home again, home again, jiggety jig.

To market, to market, to buy a fat hog.
Home again, home again, jiggety jog.

To market, to market, to buy a plum bun.
Home again, home again, market is done.

OLD BRASS WAGON
Song / Circle Game

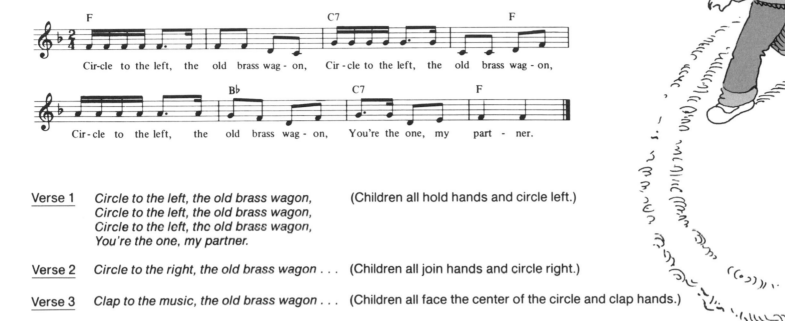

F   C7   F

Cir-cle to the left, the old brass wag-on, Cir-cle to the left, the old brass wag-on,

Bb   C7   F

Cir-cle to the left, the old brass wag-on, You're the one, my part - ner.

Verse 1   *Circle to the left, the old brass wagon,*   (Children all hold hands and circle left.)
Circle to the left, the old brass wagon,
Circle to the left, the old brass wagon,
You're the one, my partner.

Verse 2   *Circle to the right, the old brass wagon . . .*   (Children all join hands and circle right.)

Verse 3   *Clap to the music, the old brass wagon . . .*   (Children all face the center of the circle and clap hands.)

Verse 4   *Into the middle, the old brass wagon,*   (Children all join hands, walk to the center of the circle, and raise hands.)
Out of the middle, the old brass wagon,   (Children walk backward to the original circle and lower hands.)
Into the middle, the old brass wagon,   (Children all walk to the center of the circle and raise hands.)
You're the one, my partner.   (Children walk backward to the original circle and release their hands.)

You need: a piano
the assistance of your school music teacher

Steps:

1. Have children stand in a large circle. Invite the music teacher to play this song on the piano. Then teach children the words and actions.

2. Ask children to sing along as they perform the actions.

3. When children are familiar with the song, add these additional verses. Assign each child a partner. After singing verse 4, have children sing: "Swing with your partner." (Partners link right elbows and turn clockwise in circles.) "All promenade home." (Children will hold hands with partners and take gliding steps as they circle to the right.)

Variation:

Use this simple tune in a listening activity. Place various rhythm instruments on a table. Ask one child to select an instrument. Then sing the song and fill in the name of the chosen instrument. For example: "Listen to the sticks" (child plays sticks instead of singing "old brass wagon"), then on the last line, the child plays the sticks alone, following the rhythm.

BOUNCE THAT BALL!
Nonsense Rhymes / Action Games

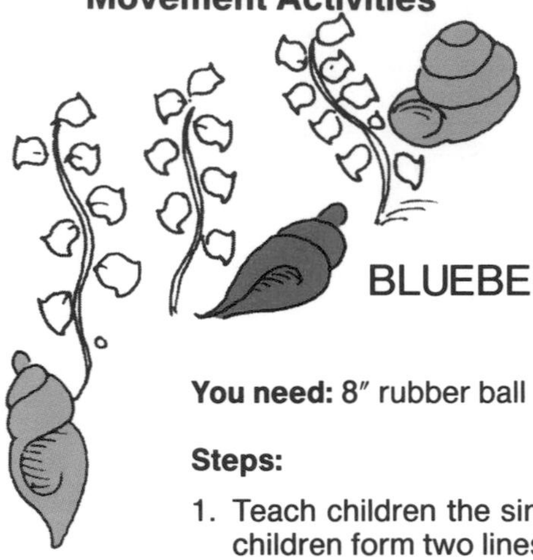

For years these children's rhymes have been passed from child to child,
changing constantly as children exchange them. Use these rhymes with activities
that involve bouncing balls or jumping rope.

BLUEBELLS, COCKLESHELLS

You need: 8″ rubber ball

Steps:

1. Teach children the simple rhyme below. On the playground, have children form two lines facing each other.

2. Give a ball to the first child in one line, who bounces it as he or she recites the rhyme. On the last *over,* the child bounces the ball to the first child in the opposite line. That child repeats the rhyme and bounces the ball, passing it to the next child in the other line.

3. Continue until each child has had a turn to bounce the ball and say the rhyme.

Variation:

For a jump rope activity, have two children gently swing a rope back and forth as another child (the jumper) stands next to it. On the last *over,* the children holding the rope will swing it over the jumper's head to begin his or her jump rope turn.

*Bluebells, cockleshells,
Eevy, ivy, over.
Bluebells, cockleshells,
The ball (rope) is coming over!*

NUMBER NONSENSE

You need: 8″ rubber ball

Steps:

1. Ask children to form two lines facing each other.

2. Give the first child in one line a ball. He or she bounces the ball and then bounces it to the child opposite as children recite the first line of the rhyme below. The children who do not have the ball do the actions (e.g., "touch your tongue").

3. Each line of the rhyme is recited in turn as another child bounces the ball.

*Number one, touch your tongue!
Number two, touch your shoe!
Number three, touch your knee!
Number four, touch the floor!
Number five, jump alive!
Number six, give some kicks!
Number seven, look to heaven!
Number eight, stand up straight!
Number nine, touch your spine!
Number ten, do it again!*

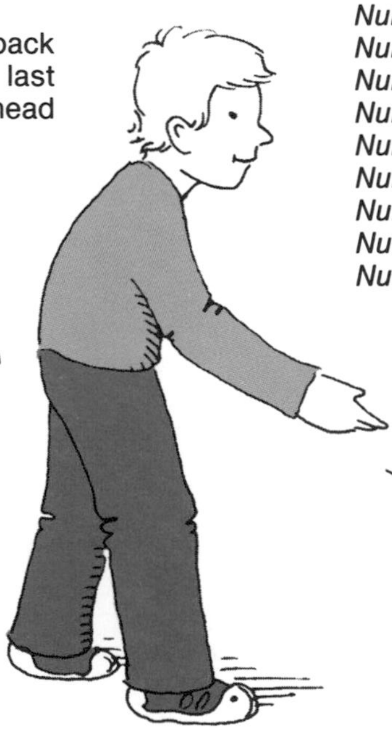

Any of the silly rhymes on this page and page 26 can be used with jump rope or ball-bouncing activities.

Cinderella, dressed in green,
Scrubbed the floors till they were clean,
How many floors did she scrub?
One, two, three, four . . .
(Continue until you miss.)

Bread and butter, sugar and spice,
How many people think I'm nice?
One, two, three, four . . .
(Continue until you miss.)

You need: two or three jump ropes or rubber balls

Steps:

1. Teach children the rhymes on this page and page 26. Then give jump ropes or rubber balls to two or three children. This group of children will jump rope or bounce the balls as they say a rhyme. The other children will clap to the rhythm of the chant.

2. When the children in the first group have finished their turns (when they have missed jumping the ropes or catching the balls), they pass the ropes or balls to other children, who begin saying a rhyme as they take their turns.

3. Continue this activity until all the children have had turns jumping rope or bouncing balls.

Variations:

1. For the rhymes that contain color words, have children substitute other colors and make up their own rhymes. For example:

    My friend, my friend, all dressed in pink,
    Tell me what time you skate at the rink.

    Cinderella, dressed in red,
    Went downstairs to bake some bread,
    How many loaves did she make?

2. With older classes, have children count by even numbers, odd numbers, or by fives and tens.

Peel a banana upside down,
Peel an orange round and round,
If you can jump (or count) to 24,
You can have your turn once more!
One, two, three, four . . .
(Continue until you miss.)

My friend, my friend, all dressed in red,
Tell me what time you go to bed.
One o'clock, two o'clock, three o'clock . . .
(Continue until you miss.)

JAZZY JINGLES
Playground Chants

Teach children the jingles on this page and page 25 to use when performing jump rope or ball-bouncing activities.

Mary, Mary, dressed in yellow,
Went upstairs to kiss her fellow,
Made a mistake and kissed a snake,
And came downstairs with a bellyache!

Johnny's got the whooping cough
Mary's got the measles
That's the way the money goes,
Pop goes the weasel!

One, two, three, four, five,
I caught a hare alive,
Six, seven, eight, nine, ten,
I let him go again.
Why did I let him go?
Because he bit my finger so!

Are you coming out, sir?
No, sir. Why, sir?
Because I've got a cold, sir.
Where'd you get the cold, sir?
At the North Pole, sir.
What were you doing there, sir?
Catching polar bears, sir.
How many did you catch, sir?
One, sir, two, sir, three, sir—
That's enough for me, sir!

Here comes the teacher yelling—
Wonder what I got in spelling!
10, 20, 30, 40, 50 . . .
(Continue until you miss.)

ANIMAL ECHOES

Rhyming Story / Body Movements

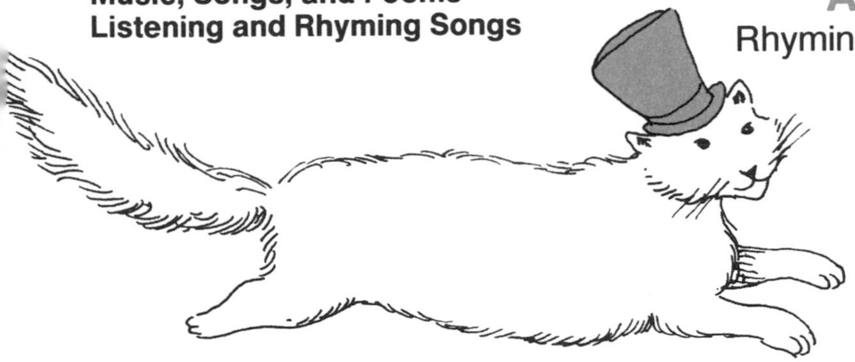

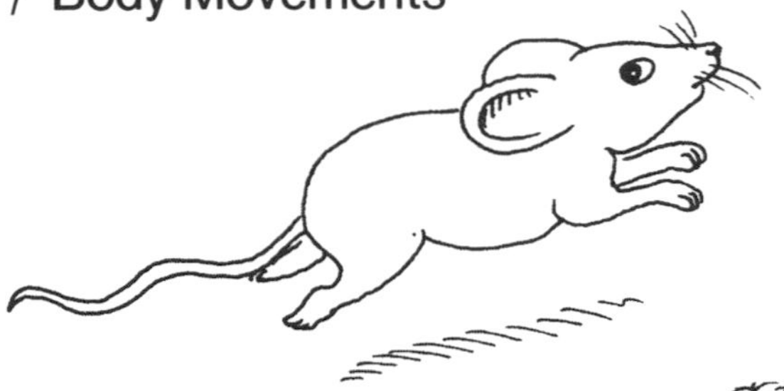

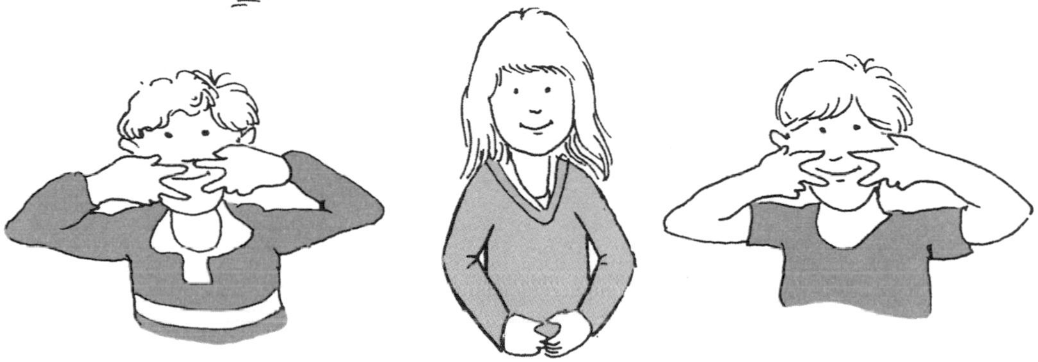

Steps:

1. Tell the children you are going to recite and act out a rhyming story.
2. They must listen to each phrase and repeat it, copying your actions as they recite each line.
3. Say the following poem, chanting it slowly and doing the actions indicated.

My pet's a cat	(Hold fingers by mouth for whiskers.)
Who's very fat.	(Make a circle in front of your stomach with your arms.)
My pet's a cat	(Hold fingers by mouth for whiskers.)
Who wears a hat.	(Hold hands in a peak over head to make a hat.)
My pet's a cat	(Hold fingers by mouth for whiskers.)
Who caught a rat.	(Raise fingers to make claws and make a mean face.)
MEOW!	(Jump forward and shout "MEOW.")

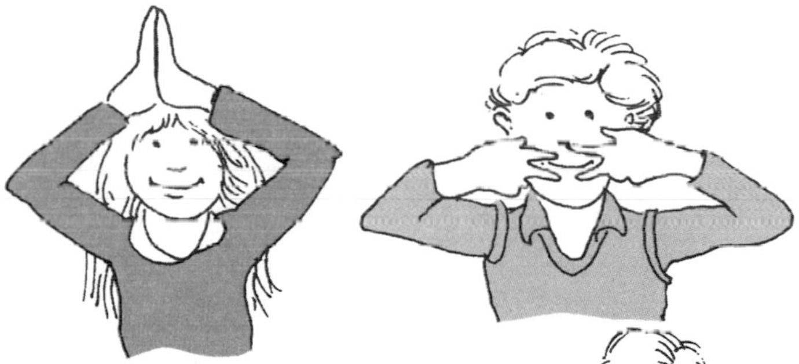

4. Then tell the story again, asking children to clap the rhythm for each line after you say it, omitting the words and actions. If desired, you may clap the rhythm for each line and have children say the words and do the actions.

Follow-up Activity:

Choose different children to be leaders and have them make up their own pet poems and actions, for example: "My pet's a pig who's very big," "My pet's a goat who wears a coat," "My pet's a frog who rides a dog," "My pet's a fish who made a wish." Echo and mimic whatever they make up. Rhymes are fun, but remind children that their poems don't have to rhyme.

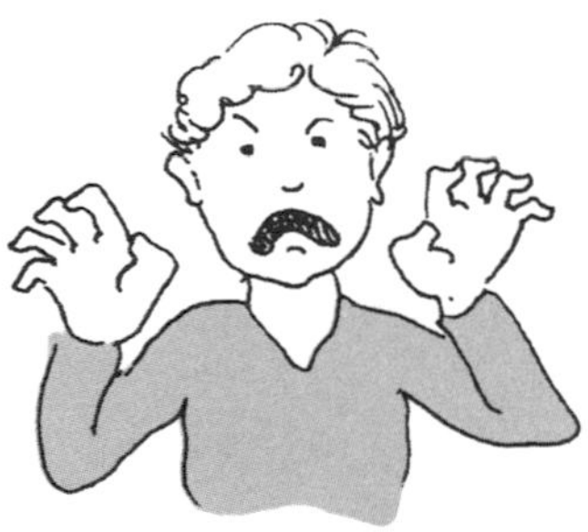

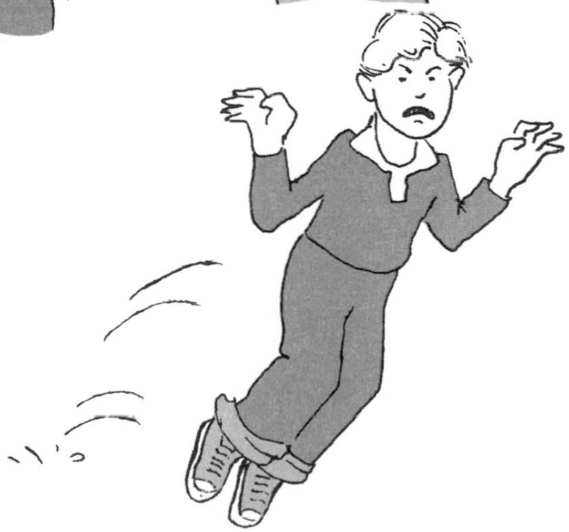

UP THE SCALE AND DOWN
Musical Scales

ASCENDING SCALE

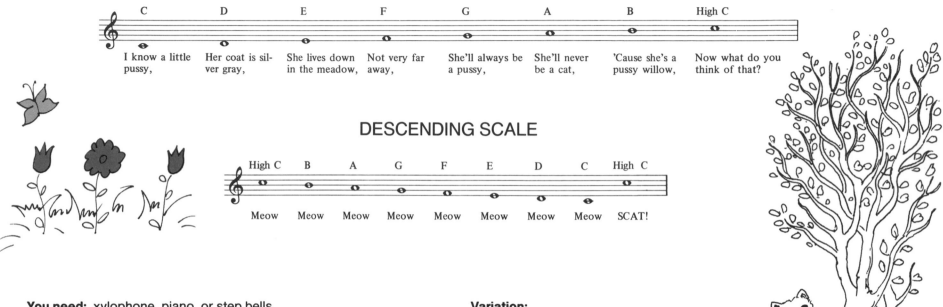

C	D	E	F	G	A	B	High C
I know a little pussy,	Her coat is sil-ver gray,	She lives down in the meadow,	Not very far away,	She'll always be a pussy,	She'll never be a cat,	'Cause she's a pussy willow,	Now what do you think of that?

DESCENDING SCALE

High C	B	A	G	F	E	D	C	High C
Meow	Meow	Meow	Meow	Meow	Meow	Meow	Meow	SCAT!

You need: xylophone, piano, or step bells

Steps:

1. Ask children to listen as you sing the first verse and demonstrate with a xylophone, piano, or step bells how each line goes up one step. Tell children this is an ascending scale, where each note is one step higher than the note before it.

2. Have the children sing the first verse with you, starting in a crouched position, and rising slightly higher as they sing each line.

3. Next, have children listen as you sing the *meow* descending scale, again playing the xylophone, piano, or bells. Ask the children whether the *meow*s go up or down.

4. Have the children stand tall and sing the *meow*s with you, squatting lower and lower as they sing each *meow*.

5. End the song with a *SCAT!* on high C and have the children jump up high.

6. Repeat, putting the whole song together.

Variation:

Substitute these lyrics as you sing the scales:

I have a little puppy,
He has a stubby tail,
He isn't very chubby,
He's skinny as a rail,
He'll always be a puppy,
He'll never be a hound,
They sell him at the butcher shop,
For 99¢ a pound.
BOW WOW WOW WOW WOW WOW WOW WOW
HOT DOG!

Follow-up Activity:

Give each child an 18″ × 24″ piece of dark construction paper. Ask each child to draw a large branch on the paper. Then have children dip their index fingers into thick white paint and make fingerprints around the branches for the pussy willows.

A-HUNTING WE WILL GO
Rhyming Song / Art Activity

Oh, a-hunt-ing we will go, a-hunt-ing we will go, We'll catch a fox and put him in a box, And then we'll let him go!

You need: 9″ × 12″ white construction paper
crayons

Steps:

1. Teach the song to the class. Ask children to add new verses by naming an animal they'd like to catch and then thinking of something to do with that animal that will rhyme with its name. For example:

   We'll catch a fish and put him in a dish.

   We'll catch a goat and put her in a boat.

   We'll catch a duck and let him drive a truck.

   We'll catch a cat and make her wear a hat.

2. After the children have had an opportunity to make and hear many rhymes, give each child a 9″ × 12″ piece of white construction paper. Ask each child to fill the paper with a picture of an animal involved in a rhyming situation (e.g., mouse in a house, cat wearing a hat, and so on). If desired, children may write the rhyming words on their papers.

3. Collect the pictures. The next time the song is sung, have each child hold up a picture to inspire a verse.

Variations:

1. Add movement to the song. Ask children to form a circle. Let the children gallop to the right as the first verse is sung. As the next verse is sung, children will turn and gallop to the left. Alternate directions with each verse.

2. Use musical instruments to give signals to change movement. Have children sing the song, walking when they hear a drum being played, skipping when they hear a tambourine, and galloping when the wood block is played. Let children take turns playing the instruments.

JOHN JACOB JINGLEHEIMER SCHMIDT
Loud and Soft Sounds

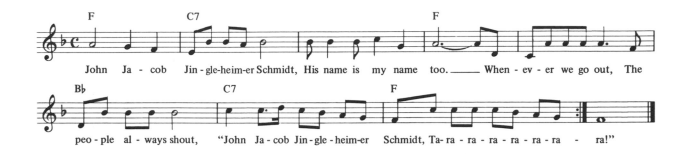

John Ja - cob Jin - gle-heim-er Schmidt, His name is my name too.___ When - ev - er we go out, The peo - ple al - ways shout, "John Ja - cob Jin - gle - heim-er Schmidt, Ta- ra - ra - ra - ra - ra - ra - ra!"

Steps:

1. Sing this song for the children.

2. Then sing it with the class, allowing children to sing extremely loudly on the *Ta-ra-ra* part at the end.

3. Repeat the song over and over, each time singing it a little softer, until you are whispering the song. However, each time the *Ta-ra-ra* part is sung it remains loud.

Variation:

When children are familiar with this song, have the class stand in a circle. Choose one child to be the leader. Give the leader a drum and ask him or her to sing the song and march around the circle beating the drum. On the *Ta-ra-ra* part, the leader stops and stands behind a child in the circle. The song is sung again, as that child follows the leader around the circle. Repeat the song until all the children are marching behind the leader.

Follow-up Activities:

These other activities also make children aware of loud and soft sounds.

1. Beat a drum softly and have children tiptoe around the room. Then beat the drum loudly and have them stomp around the room. Give each child a turn to play the drum softly or loudly.

2. Give each child a piece of drawing paper and some crayons. Beat a drum softly or play soft music and have children draw "soft" pictures on one side of their papers. On the other side of their papers, ask the children to draw "loud" pictures as you play loud music or beat a drum loudly.

A RAM-SAM-SAM
Moroccan Song / Hand Motions

A ram-sam-sam, a ram-sam-sam, Gu-li gu-li gu-li gu-li gu-li ram-sam-sam. A-ra-fi, a-ra-fi, Gu-li gu-li gu-li gu-li gu-li ram-sam-sam.

You need: a piano
the assistance of your school music teacher

Steps:

1. Have children sit in a circle on the floor. Have the music teacher play the song on the piano for the class.

2. Teach children the words and corresponding hand motions, and let them sing along as they do the actions.

First line:

A ram-sam-sam (pronounced "a rum-sum-sum"), a ram-sam-sam,

Second line:

Guli (pronounced "goolie") guli guli guli guli ram-sam-sam.

Third line:

Arafi (pronounced "a-ra' -fee"), arafi,

Fourth line:

Guli guli guli guli guli ram-sam-sam.

Variation:

Older classes may sing this song as a round. Divide the class into two groups, and have the second group begin the song after the first group completes the second line.

Hand Motions:

1. On *ram,* children will clap their hands.

2. Each time *sam* is sung, children will make fists with their thumbs pointing down.

3. Whenever *guli* is sung, children will rotate their hands over each other repeatedly.

4. On *ara-*, children will raise both hands and shake them.

5. On *-fi,* children will slap their laps with both hands.

BINGO AND VARIATIONS
Clapping Song

There was a farm-er had a dog and Bin-go was his name, oh! B - I - N - G - O,

B - I - N - G - O! B - I - N - G - O, and Bin-go was his name, oh!

Steps:

1. Teach the song to the class.

2. Then repeat the song, instructing children to leave out the letter *B* and clap once in its place.

3. Sing the song again, this time having children leave out the letters *B* and *I*, clapping in their places.

4. Repeat the song, each time leaving out one more letter of the dog's name and adding one more clap. Before singing each verse, you may want to hold up the appropriate number of fingers to indicate to children how many times they are to clap.

5. On the final verse the children should not say any letters. Instead, they will clap five times in rhythm with the music.

Variations:

1. Substitute other five-letter names to make new holiday songs. For example:

   There was a man with a great big pack and Santa was his name, ho!

   There was a house that had a ghost and Henry was his name, boo!

   There was a witch who rode a broom and Wanda was her name, oh!

   A Pilgrim had an Indian friend and Eagle was his name, how!

   Let children suggest other characters' names.

2. Distribute rhythm instruments (drums, bells, triangles, wood blocks, maracas) to children. Ask children to play the instruments instead of clapping hands as they sing the song.

BILL GROGAN'S GOAT
Echo Song

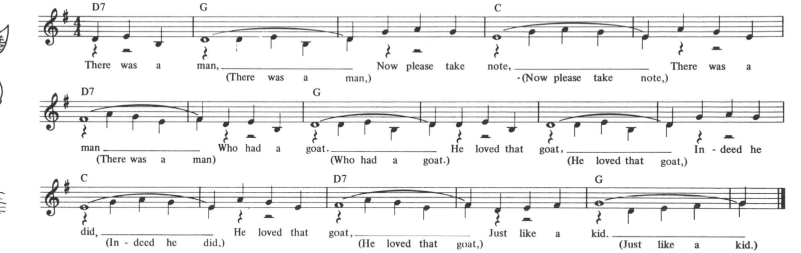

There was a man, _____ Now please take note, _____ There was a
(There was a man,) ·(Now please take note,)

man _____ Who had a goat. _____ He loved that goat, _____ In - deed he
(There was a man) (Who had a goat.) (He loved that goat,)

did, _____ He loved that goat, _____ Just like a kid.
(In - deed he did,) (He loved that goat,) (Just like a kid.)

Verse 1

There was a man, (echo each phrase)
Now please take note,
There was a man
Who had a goat.
He loved that goat,
Indeed he did,
He loved that goat,
Just like a kid.

Verse 2

One day that goat
Felt frisky and fine,
Ate three nice shirts,
Right off the line.
The man, he grabbed
Him by the back,
And tied him to
A railroad track.

Verse 3

Now, when that train
Drove into sight,
That goat grew pale,
And green with fright.
He heaved a sigh,
As if in pain,
Coughed up those shirts
And flagged the train.

Steps:

1. Teach this song to children by singing a phrase and having children repeat the phrase as written in the music above.

2. As the children become more familiar with the song, select a lead singer from the group to sing the song for other children to echo.

Follow-up Activity:

Reproduce the worksheet on page 34 for each child. Have each child glue a piece of colored yarn from one tree to the other on the worksheet to make the clothesline. Show children how to cut out a shirt in the shape of a *T*. Next, ask each child to cut three shirts out of wallpaper or fabric scraps and glue them just below the clothesline, letting the goat munch on one of them. Then have children color their worksheets.

BILL GROGAN'S GOAT
Worksheet

Name_____

Down by the bay, _____ Where the wa-ter-mel-ons grow, _____ Back to my
(Down by the bay,) (Where the wa-ter-mel-ons grow,)

home, _____ I dare not go. _____ For if I do, _____ My mo-ther will
(Back to my home,) (I dare not go.) (For if I do,)

say, _____ "Did you ev-er see a bear comb-ing his hair, Down by the bay?"
(My mo-ther will say,)

Suggested Rhymes:

Did you ever see a bee with a donkey on his knee?

Did you ever see a moose playing with a goose?

Did you ever see a deer with one purple ear?

Did you ever see a bear inside a yellow pear?

Did you ever see a monkey riding on a donkey?

Did you ever see a giraffe sit down and laugh?

You need: pictures of various animals

Steps:

1. Teach children the song on this page by singing each phrase and having children echo the phrase. Then tell the children that they will be creating their own silly rhymes for this song.

2. To give children the idea, sing the song with them several times, substituting some of the suggested rhymes at the right after the phrase "My mother will say."

3. Give each child an animal picture. Ask each child to make up a silly rhyme using the name of the animal in the picture. Give children a few minutes to think of their rhymes.

4. When children have thought of their silly rhymes, tell the class that you will point to a child during the song. The child you point to must say or sing his or her rhyme after the phrase "My mother will say." Repeat the song until each child has had a turn.

Music, Songs, and Poems
Concept Songs
Body Awareness

OPEN, SHUT THEM
Song / Hand Motions

page 36

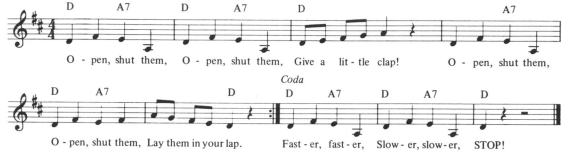

O - pen, shut them, O - pen, shut them, Give a lit - tle clap! O - pen, shut them,

Coda

O - pen, shut them, Lay them in your lap. Fast - er, fast - er, Slow - er, slow - er, STOP!

Verse 1

Open, shut them,	(Hold your hands out, palms facing away from you,
Open, shut them,	and spread fingers open, then close them in a fist.)
Give a little clap!	(Clap once.)
Open, shut them,	(Open and shut your fingers.)
Open, shut them,	
Lay them in your lap.	(Place both hands in your lap.)
Creep them, crawl them,	(Creep your fingers upward from your lap until
Creep them, crawl them,	they reach your chin.)
Right up to your chin.	
Open wide your little mouth,	(Open mouth.)
But do not let them in.	(Quickly put hands behind your back.)

Verse 2

Open, shut them,	(Open and shut your fingers.)
Open, shut them,	
To your shoulders fly.	(Flutter your fingers up to your shoulders.)
Then like little birdies let them	(Flutter your fingers as you wave your hands
Flutter to the sky.	upward to the ceiling.)
Falling, falling,	(Flutter your fingers as you move your hands down
Falling, falling,	toward the ground.)
Almost to the ground.	
Quickly pick them up again.	(Move your hands up in front of you.)
And turn them round and round.	(Rotate hands over one another.)
Faster, faster,	(Rotate hands faster and faster.)
Slower, slower,	(Rotate hands slower and slower.)
STOP!	(Put hands, palms out, to indicate "stop.")

You need: a piano
the assistance of your school
music teacher

Steps:

1. Invite the music teacher to play this song on the piano for the class. Then teach children the first verse of this song and the accompanying actions. After children have sung this verse several times, introduce the second verse and its actions.

2. Let children sing along as they perform the actions.

3. Use this song to get children's attention when they become too noisy or unattentive. Begin to sing the song, not following the words. For example, when you sing "Right up to your chin," move your fingers up to the top of your head. Ask children to watch closely and correct you when you make an incorrect motion.

Music, Songs, and Poems
Concept Songs
Body Awareness

WIGGLY SONG
Action Song

page 37

My thumbs are start-ing to wig-gle, My thumbs are start-ing to wig-gle, My thumbs are start-ing to wig-gle, A-round, a-round, a-round.___

Verse 2

My thumbs and fingers are wiggling . . .

Verse 3

My hands are starting to wiggle . . .

Verse 4

My arms are starting to wiggle . . .

Verse 5

My head is starting to wiggle . . . .

Verse 6

Now all of me is wiggling,
Now all of me is wiggling,
Now all of me is wiggling,
And then I sit right down!

You need: a piano
the assistance of your school music teacher

Steps:

1. Ask students to stand in a circle. Invite the music teacher to play this song on the piano, and teach children the words.

2. This song is sung to the tune of "The Bear Went Over the Mountain." Have children sing along as they wiggle their thumbs. As each verse is sung, children will continue wiggling the body parts previously mentioned. At the end of the song, children will sit down.

3. When the children are sitting, you will have their attention to begin a listening activity.

4. Sing the song again, and vary the order of body parts—first the head, then the arms, and so on. Children must listen carefully in order to know which parts of their bodies should be wiggling.

Music, Songs, and Poems
Concept Songs
Body Awareness

AIKEN DRUM
Silly Song

page 38

There_ was a man lived in the moon, lived in the moon, lived
And he played up-on a la - dle, a la - dle, a

in the moon. There_ was a man lived in the moon and his name was Ai - ken Drum.
la - dle, And he played up-on a la - dle, and his name was Ai - ken Drum.

You need: soup ladle with 6″ string tied to it
spoon

Optional: large piece of chart paper
markers

Steps:

1. Tell the children you are going to teach them a silly song about a man who lived in the moon. This man's name was Aiken Drum and he was made up of all different kinds of foods. His hair, his arms, and the rest of his body were all made up of your favorite foods.

2. Sing the first verse, then sing it again, asking children to sing along:

   There was a man lived in the moon, lived in the moon, lived in the moon,
   There was a man lived in the moon and his name was Aiken Drum.

3. Tell the children Aiken Drum used a special instrument to help him sing his song. Show them the ladle. Holding the ladle by the string, hit it with the spoon on the first beat of each measure as you sing the chorus. Then sing the chorus again, asking the children to sing with you.

   Chorus:

   And he played upon a ladle, a ladle, a ladle,
   And he played upon a ladle, and his name was Aiken Drum.

4. Now ask the children to help you make up the rest of the song. Repeat the first verse and chorus. Then create Aiken Drum. Sing:

   And his hair was made of _____ (ask children to name a food),
   Of _____ , of _____ ,
   And his hair was made of _____ ,
   And his name was Aiken Drum.

5. Sing the chorus, giving the ladle and spoon to a child to play on the first beat of every measure. After the chorus, ask one child to name the food to make the next part of Aiken Drum's body. Add other verses, describing Aiken Drum's eyes, nose, ears, mouth, and so on. Let individual children suggest foods to make Aiken Drum's body parts. Sing the chorus after each verse, passing the ladle to a different child each time.

6. If desired, draw a picture of Aiken Drum on large chart paper as children sing the song.

Variations:

1. Have children use other kitchen utensils as instruments: pots, lids, cheese graters and spoon, strainer and spoon, wooden spoons, and so on.

2. Ask older children to name only fruits for Aiken Drum's body. Vary with only dairy products, vegetables, breakfast foods, and so on.

Follow-up Activities:

1. Have each child draw his or her own version of Aiken Drum after the song is sung.

2. Let children cut out pictures of food from old magazines to paste on simple body outlines to create Aiken Drum.

IF YOU'RE HAPPY AND YOU KNOW IT
Action Song

Verse 1

If you're happy and you know it, clap your hands (clap clap),
If you're happy and you know it, clap your hands (clap clap),
If you're happy and you know it, then your face will surely show it,
If you're happy and you know it, clap your hands (clap clap).

Verse 2

If you're happy and you know it, stamp your feet (stamp stamp),
If you're happy and you know it, stamp your feet (stamp stamp),
If you're happy and you know it, then your face will surely show it,
If you're happy and you know it, stamp your feet (stamp stamp).

Steps:

1. Teach your class this song, asking children to do the actions indicated.

2. Add other verses, such as tap your head, touch your toes, slap your legs, pull your ears, bend your knees, and shake your arms.

3. When children are familiar with the song, sing it again, leaving out the action words as you do the actions in time to the music.

Variation:

Distribute various percussion instruments (drums, bells, tambourines, maracas) to children. Sing the song, substituting instructions to play a specific instrument for the action words. For example, sing: "If you're happy and you know it, play the drum." Only those children who have the named instrument will play their instruments. Let children exchange instruments after you have sung several verses.

DO YOUR EARS HANG LOW?
Silly Song / Hand Motions

Do your ears hang low? Do they wob-ble to and fro? Can you tie 'em in a knot? Can you

tie 'em in a bow? Can you throw 'em o'er your shoul-der like a con-ti-nen-tal sol-dier? Do your ears hang low?

Do your ears hang low?	(Place thumbs on ears, with fingers pointing down.)
Do they wobble to and fro?	(Wave fingers, keeping thumbs on ears.)
Can you tie 'em in a knot?	(Rotate hands over one another.)
Can you tie 'em in a bow?	(Rotate hands in the other direction and pull them apart as if tying a bow.)
Can you throw 'em o'er your shoulder	(Toss both hands over one shoulder.)
Like a continental soldier?	(Salute like a soldier.)
Do your ears hang low?	(Place thumbs on ears with fingers pointing down.)

Steps:

1. Teach this silly song to your class, asking children to mimic you as you do the hand motions indicated.

2. When children are familiar with the song, let them make up additional verses and motions using other body parts ("Do your arms wave high?" "Do your knees bend low?" and so on).

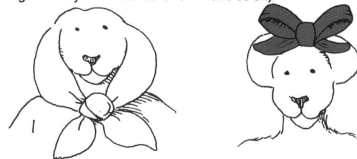

Variation:

Teach children this alternate version:
Do your ears hang high?
    (Place thumbs on ears, with fingers pointing up.)
Do they reach up to the sky?
    (Raise both hands up in the air.)
Can they wiggle to say hi?
    (Pull ears and shake them, then wave with one hand.)
Can they wobble to say bye?
    (Pull ears and shake them, then wave with other hand.)
Can you throw 'em o'er your shoulder
    (Toss both hands over one shoulder.)
Like a continental soldier?
    (Salute like a soldier.)
Do your ears hang high?
    (Place thumbs on ears, with fingers pointing up.)

Music, Songs, and Poems
Concept Songs
Numbers and Counting

ONE IN THE BED
Counting Song

page 41

F

There was one in the bed, and the lit-tle one said, "I'm lone-ly, I'm

lone-ly!" So he rolled o-ver and one jumped in.

You need: a piano
the assistance of your school music teacher

Optional: quilt or blanket

Steps:

1. Have children sit in a large circle. Invite your music teacher to play the song on the piano, and teach children the words.

2. If desired, lay a quilt or blanket on the floor in the center of the circle to represent a bed. Select five children. Choose one child to be the "little one." Assign the other four children numbers from 2 to 5. The children with assigned numbers sit in the circle, and the "little one" lies down in the center of the circle.

3. Everyone sings the song. Those forming the circle may use the hand motions suggested in the variation. Allow the "little one" to sing the words "I'm lonely, I'm lonely" by himself or herself. At these words, the child whose number is 2 will go to the center of the circle and lie down next to the "little one."

4. Continue the song and actions in the same manner, each time adding one child to those in the bed until there are five children lying in the center of the circle.

5. When there are five in the bed, the song's action reverses. During subsequent verses, the fifth, fourth, third, and second children roll away from the "little one" and go back to the circle. The song concludes with:

There was one in the bed and the little one said, "Good night!"

Variation:

Sing this song using hand motions. Hold up the appropriate number of fingers to show how many are in the bed, wiggle the pinkie when the "little one" talks, rotate the hands over each other at the words *roll over*, hold up one finger for *one*, slap lap for *jumped* and *fell*, and clap for *in* and *out*.

Music, Songs, and Poems
Concept Songs
Numbers and Counting

ONE IN THE BED
Art Activity   Visual Aid

page 42

You need: half-sheets of shirt cardboard about 7″ × 8″
(one for each child)
3″ × 6″ fabric scraps (one for each child)
glue
7″ × 8″ pieces of construction paper
straight clothespins or ice-cream sticks
(five for each child)
fine-line markers
yarn scraps or cotton

Steps:

1. Give each child a piece of cardboard and a piece of fabric.

2. Ask each child to glue a 7″ × 8″ piece of construction paper onto the cardboard. Let dry.

3. Instruct each child to place the fabric scrap horizontally on the lower half of the cardboard. Each child will glue the bottom edge and the two short sides of the fabric onto the cardboard. Leave the top edge open. This is the blanket on the bed.

4. Next, give each child five clothespins or ice-cream sticks. With markers, have each child draw faces on the heads of the clothespins or the ends of the ice-cream sticks.

5. To make hair for the clothespin or ice-cream-stick people, children will glue a few scraps of yarn or cotton around the faces.

6. Then have each child tuck one clothespin person under the blanket so that the head shows.

7. Instead of acting out the song "One in the Bed," each child will add one person to the bed each time the words "one jumped in" are sung. When the words "one fell out" are sung, the child will remove one person from the bed. Thus each child can visualize the addition and subtraction processes described in the song.

8. If desired, have children complete the bedroom of their clothespin or ice-cream-stick people by drawing toy shelves, pictures, headboards, and so on, on their pictures.

Variation:

Simply give each child five ice-cream sticks. Have children draw clothes and features on the sticks with markers. Children may lay the stick people in front of them, using their desks as the beds and manipulating the stick people as the song is sung.

Music, Songs, and Poems
Concept Songs
Numbers and Counting

THIS OLD MAN
Counting Song / Hand and Body Motions

page 43

Verse 1

This old man, he played one,
He played nick-nack on my thumb,

Chorus

With a nick-nack, paddy wack, give the dog a bone,
This old man came rolling home.

Verse 2

This old man, he played two . . . on my shoe.

Verse 3

This old man, he played three . . . on my knee.

Verse 4

This old man, he played four . . . on my door.

Verse 5

This old man, he played five . . . on my hive.

Verse 6

This old man, he played six . . . on my sticks.

Verse 7

This old man, he played seven . . . up in heaven.

Verse 8

This old man, he played eight . . . on my gate.

Verse 9

This old man, he played nine . . . on my spine.

Verse 10

This old man, he played ten . . . once again.

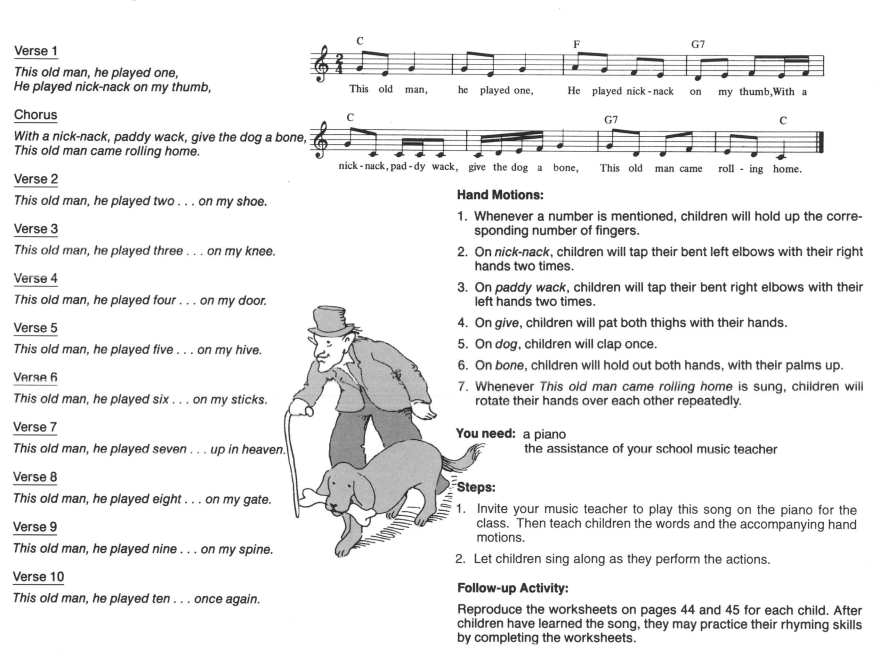

Hand Motions:

1. Whenever a number is mentioned, children will hold up the corresponding number of fingers.

2. On *nick-nack*, children will tap their bent left elbows with their right hands two times.

3. On *paddy wack*, children will tap their bent right elbows with their left hands two times.

4. On *give*, children will pat both thighs with their hands.

5. On *dog*, children will clap once.

6. On *bone*, children will hold out both hands, with their palms up.

7. Whenever *This old man came rolling home* is sung, children will rotate their hands over each other repeatedly.

You need: a piano
the assistance of your school music teacher

Steps:

1. Invite your music teacher to play this song on the piano for the class. Then teach children the words and the accompanying hand motions.

2. Let children sing along as they perform the actions.

Follow-up Activity:

Reproduce the worksheets on pages 44 and 45 for each child. After children have learned the song, they may practice their rhyming skills by completing the worksheets.

Music, Songs, and Poems
Concept Songs
Numbers and Counting

THIS OLD MAN
Rhyming Worksheet

page 44

Cut out the pictures in the bottom row on this page.
Paste each picture in the box below the numeral it rhymes with.
To help you, think of the rhyming words in the song "This Old Man."

Name _____

Music, Songs, and Poems
Concept Songs
Numbers and Counting

THIS OLD MAN
Rhyming Worksheet

page 45

Cut out the pictures in the bottom row on this page.
Paste each picture in the box below the numeral it rhymes with.
To help you, think of the rhyming words in the song "This Old Man."

Name _____

JOHNNY WORKS WITH ONE HAMMER
Counting Song / Hand and Body Motions

John - ny works with one ham - mer, one ham - mer, one ham - mer,

John - ny works with one ham - mer, then he works with two.

You need: a piano
the assistance of your school music teacher

Steps:

1. Invite your music teacher to play this song on the piano for the class. Have children sit in chairs in a circle, and teach them the song.

2. Have children sing the first verse, asking them to keep the beat as they sing by hammering their right fists on their right knees.

3. For the second verse, children will sing, "Johnny works with two hammers . . ." and add another motion, hammering on their left knees with their fists.

4. Sing the third verse, "Johnny works with three hammers . . ." and ask children to tap the floor with their right feet as they hammer their knees with their fists.

5. For the fourth verse, "Johnny works with four hammers . . ." have children add the motions of tapping their left feet on the floor.

6. Sing the fifth verse, "Johnny works with five hammers . . ." and ask children to nod their heads up and down to the beat as they do the other actions. Conclude this verse with "then he works no more."

Variations:

1. Choose five percussion instruments: wood block, drum, sticks, tambourine, and triangle or cymbal. Choose a child to play one instrument as the class sings verse 1. Select another child to play a second instrument as the second verse is sung. Continue to add a new instrument with each verse.

2. Write the numerals 1 to 5 on large cards. Place the cards on the floor in the center of the circle. As each verse is sung, choose a child to find and hold up the appropriate numbered card.

Music, Songs, and Poems
Concept Songs
Numbers and Counting

THE ANTS GO MARCHING
Action Song

page 47

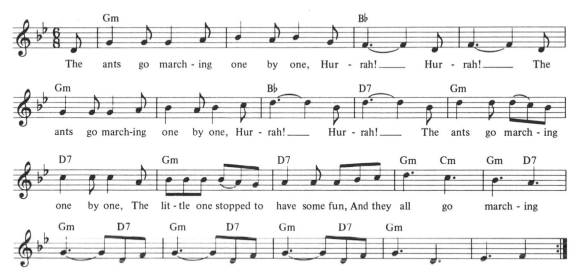

The ants go march-ing one by one, Hur-rah!___ Hur-rah!___ The ants go march-ing one by one, Hur-rah!___ Hur-rah!___ The ants go march-ing one by one, The lit-tle one stopped to have some fun, And they all go march-ing Down___ in the ground___ to get out___ of the rain. Tramp, tramp, tramp.

Verse 2
. . . two by two . . .
The little one stopped to tie its shoe.

Verse 3
. . . three by three . . .
The little one stopped to climb a tree.

Verse 4
. . . four by four . . .
The little one stopped to shut the door.

Verse 5
. . . five by five . . .
The little one stopped by a pool to dive.

Verse 6
. . . six by six . . .
The little one stopped to pick up sticks.

Verse 7
. . . seven by seven . . .
The little one stopped and prayed to heaven.

Verse 8
. . . eight by eight . . .
The little one stopped to open the gate.

Verse 9
. . . nine by nine . . .
The little one stopped to draw a line.

Verse 10
. . . ten by ten . . .
The little one said, "This is the end."

Steps:

1. Teach the class this song, which is sung to the tune of "When Johnny Comes Marching Home Again." Have children stand in a circle. If there are 20 or more children, have them form two circles.

2. Choose one child to be the first ant and ask him or her to march around the outside of the circle as the song is sung.

3. At the end of each verse, the child who is the first ant stops and taps another child on the shoulder. Each child who is tapped will leave the circle to follow the first ant, marching behind him or her.

4. The children remaining in the circle will march in place and panto-mime the action described in each verse (tie a shoe, climb a tree, and so on).

Follow-up Activity:

After singing the song with your class, make copies of the worksheets on pages 48 and 49 for each child. Have children complete the work-sheets to practice counting and writing skills.

THE ANTS GO MARCHING
Counting Worksheet

Name_____

Cut out the pictures on this page.
Count the ants in each picture.
Paste each picture in the box below the correct numeral.
Then trace over each numeral.

Music, Songs, and Poems
Concept Songs
Numbers and Counting

THE ANTS GO MARCHING
Counting Worksheet

page 49

Name_____

Cut out the pictures on this page.
Count the ants in each picture.
Paste each picture in the box below the correct numeral.
Then trace over each numeral.

Verse 1

Nobody likes me, ev'rybody hates me,
Guess I'll go eat worms,
Long, thin, slimy ones, short, fat, juicy ones,
Itsy-bitsy, fuzzy-wuzzy worms.

Verse 2

Down goes the first one, down goes the second one,
Oh, how they wiggle and squirm,
Long, thin, slimy ones, short, fat, juicy ones,
Itsy-bitsy, fuzzy-wuzzy worms.

Verse 3

Nobody knows how I survive on
Worms three times a day!
Long, thin, slimy ones, short, fat, juicy ones,
Itsy-bitsy, fuzzy-wuzzy worms.

Steps:

1. Before teaching your class this silly song, hold a serious discussion with children about feelings. Here are some motivating questions:

   a. What do you do to make your mother (father, sister, or brother) happy?

   b. What have you ever done to make your mother (father, sister, or brother) really angry with you? What has she (or he) ever done to make you really angry?

   c. When someone is very angry with you, how do you make that person stop being angry? Have you ever done something silly to cheer up the person who is angry with you and help that person forgive you?

   d. Doesn't it feel good when someone forgives you, or when you forgive someone you're angry with?

2. Explain to children that you are going to teach them a silly song about a boy who thinks that people don't like him, so he pretends to do something very silly to make those people laugh. Then teach the song, one verse at a time, to the class.

A PEANUT SAT ON A RAILROAD TRACK
Song / Peanut-Butter Recipe / Art Activity

A peanut sat on a railroad track,
His heart was all a-flutter.
Round the bend came Number Ten
Toot! Toot! Peanut butter! SQUISH!

(Sit cross-legged in a circle.)
(Cross hands over heart and beat chest.)
(Make a large circle with one hand, then hold up ten fingers.)
(Pull imaginary chord twice on *Toot! Toot!*, then clap and rub hands together on *SQUISH*.)

Steps:

1. Ask children to sit cross-legged in a circle.

2. Teach your class this silly song and the accompanying hand motions.

3. As follow-up activities, let children help prepare the peanut-butter recipe and do the art activity described on this page.

HOMEMADE PEANUT BUTTER

Ingredients: bag of unshelled peanuts
vegetable oil (preferably peanut oil)
celery sticks or crackers

How to make:

1. Give each child 10 peanuts to shell. (Ask the children to save the shells to use in the peanut creature activity.)

2. For each cupful of peanuts, add four teaspoons of oil.

3. Place the mixture in a blender and purée until fairly smooth.

4. Spread on celery sticks or crackers. (One cup of shelled peanuts makes two-thirds of a cup of peanut butter—enough spread for 24 crackers.)

PEANUT CREATURES

You need: animal cutouts on page 52
scissors
glue
8″ × 6″ pieces of construction paper
crushed peanut shells (from preparing the peanut-butter recipe)
peppercorns or small buttons
scraps of red yarn

Steps:

1. Make several copies of the animal cutouts on page 52.

2. Cut out the animals along the dotted lines. Have each child choose a picture.

3. Ask children to glue their animal cutouts onto 8″ × 6″ pieces of construction paper.

4. Each child will spread a thin layer of glue over the entire area inside the outline of the animal.

5. Next, have each child press the crushed peanut shells onto the glued area to make a coat for the animal.

6. Children may glue on peppercorns or small buttons for the animals' eyes. To make mouths, children can glue scraps of red yarn onto the animals.

TRICKY TONGUE TWISTERS
Make a Minibook

Color the pictures on this page.
Cut them out along the dotted lines.
Staple the pictures together to make a minibook.
Read and practice saying these tricky tongue twisters.

A skunk sat on a stump.
The stump thunk the skunk stunk.
The skunk thunk the stump stunk.

Swan swam over the sea.
Swim, swan, swim;
Swan swam back again,
Well swum, swan!

How much wood would a woodchuck chuck
If a woodchuck could chuck wood?

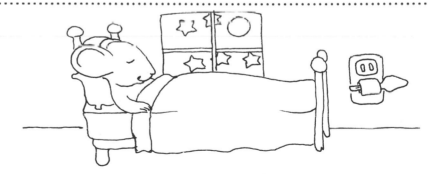

There's no need to light a night light
On a light night like tonight;
For a night light is a slight light
On a light night like tonight.

INSIDE OUT AND UPSIDE DOWN
Nonsense Rhymes / Poem Starters

You need: poem starters
scissors
glue
3″ × 5″ unlined index cards
writing paper
pencils
crayons

Steps:

1. In advance, reproduce the poem starters on this page several times.

2. Cut out the poem starters and glue each one onto a 3″ × 5″ unlined index card.

3. Teach your class the silly rhymes on this page. Then tell children that they will be making up their own silly rhymes.

4. Give each child a poem-starter card, writing paper, a pencil, and some crayons. Ask each child to think of a silly rhyme, two to four lines long, that goes with the poem starter, and write it on his or her paper. Each child may then draw a picture to illustrate the silly rhyme.

5. Let children read their silly rhymes to the class.

HEADS UP!

As I was going out one day,
My head fell off and rolled away,
But when I saw that it was gone,
I picked it up and put it on.

And when I walked on down the street,
A fellow cried: "Look at your feet!"
I looked for them and sadly said:
"I've left them both asleep in bed!"

FLOATING IN AIR

I wish that my room had a floor!
I don't so much care for a door,
But this crawling around
Without touching the ground
Is getting to be quite a bore!

If the school were made of candy . . .

If chickens learned to read and write . . .

If a pony drove a car . . .

Suppose that stars shone in the sea . . .

If pigs wore slippers on their feet . . .

Suppose a fish lived in a nest . . .

NEVER ENOUGH NONSENSE

Worksheet

Read the silly poems below out loud. On the lines at the right side of the page, write your own nonsense poem. You may begin your poem with the first line from one of the poems on this page.
In the blank space below your poem, draw a picture to go with it.

I asked my mother for fifteen cents
To see the elephant jump the fence.
He jumped so high that he touched the sky
And never came back till the Fourth of July.

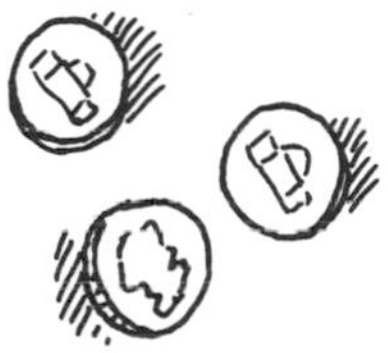

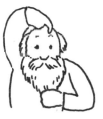

If all the world were apple pie
And all the sea were ink,
And all the trees were bread and cheese,
What would we have to drink?
It's enough to make an old man
Scratch his head and think!

Me, myself, and I—
We went to the kitchen and ate a pie.
Then my mother—she came in,
And chased us out with a rolling pin.

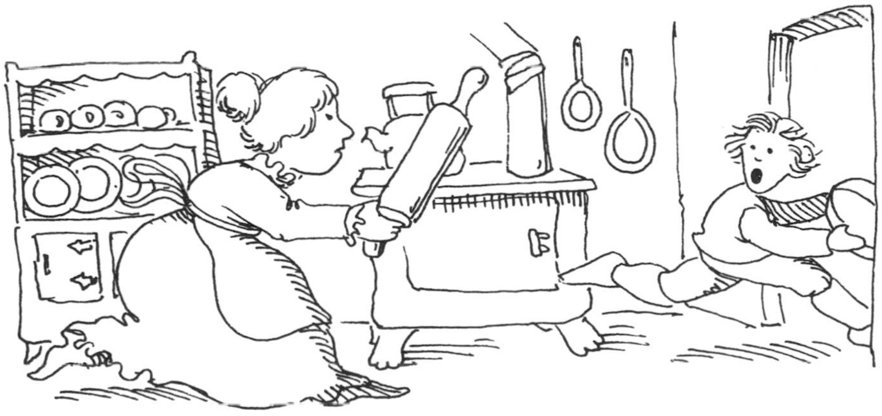

MY OWN NONSENSE

By ______________________________

____

____

____

____

____

____

____

____

THE GOBLIN IN THE DARK
Halloween Song

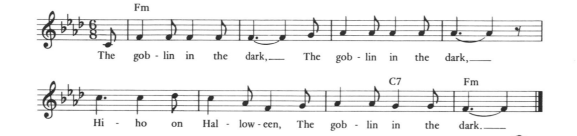

The gob - lin in the dark,___ The gob - lin in the dark,___

Hi - ho on Hal - low - een, The gob - lin in the dark.___

Steps:

1. Teach children this Halloween song, which is sung to the tune of "The Farmer in the Dell" in a minor key.

2. Have children stand in a large circle. Choose one child to be the "goblin," and ask him or her to stand in the center of the circle.

3. Ask children to begin the song. On the first two lines of each verse, children will all clap to the beat. On the last two lines of each verse, the child or children in the center will skip or glide around the circle.

4. At the end of the first verse, the goblin takes the hand of a child and brings him or her to the center of the circle. At the end of each subsequent verse, the last child chosen to come to the center of the circle will select another child to join the others who are already there.

5. If children are in costume, have them create additional verses using the names of the characters they represent before singing the final verse.

Variation:

In winter, have children sing the following song as they line up one at a time for lunch, recess, or dismissal.

The snowman stands alone,   The snowman picks a friend,   The friend picks a friend . . .
The snowman stands alone,   The snowman picks a friend,
Hi-ho it's wintertime,   Hi-ho it's wintertime,   They all march away . . .
The snowman stands alone.   The snowman picks a friend.

Verse 1

The goblin in the dark,
The goblin in the dark,
Hi-ho on Halloween,
The goblin in the dark.

Verse 2

The goblin takes a ghost,
The goblin takes a ghost,
Hi-ho on Halloween,
The goblin takes a ghost.

Verse 3

The ghost takes a witch . . .

Verse 4

The witch takes a cat . . .

Verse 5

The cat takes a bat . . .

Final Verse

They all tiptoe home,
They all tiptoe home,
Hi-ho on Halloween,
They all tiptoe home. BOO!

Sing this song with your class as Thanksgiving draws near. Variations for Halloween and St. Patrick's Day songs are provided on page 58.

Five fat turkeys	(Hold up five fingers.)
Sitting on a gate.	(Place other hand horizontally below the five fingers.)
The first one said,	(Wiggle thumb.)
"Oh, my, it's getting late!"	(Put hands on cheeks and shake head.)
The second one said,	(Wiggle index finger.)
"Thanksgiving is near."	(Put hands in prayer position.)
The third one said,	(Wiggle middle finger.)
"That makes me shake with fear."	(Shake all over.)
The fourth one said,	(Wiggle ring finger.)
"Let's run and run and run."	(Move fingers in running motion.)
The fifth one said,	(Wiggle little finger.)
"Here's the farmer with his gun."	(Aim imaginary gun.)
"Let's have turkey dinner,"	(Rub stomach with hand as if hungry.)
They heard the farmer say,	
And the five fat turkeys	(Hold up five fingers.)
Flew far away!	(Wave hand in flying motion and hide hand behind back.)

Steps:

1. This song may be sung or recited. Teach children the accompanying finger plays.

2. Have the entire class sing or recite the words as the children do the motions. If desired, choose five children to sing or say each turkey's part, with the other children filling in the rest of the song.

FIVE FAT TURKEYS AND VARIATIONS
Thanksgiving Song / Finger Plays

Teach children the words and actions to these Halloween and St. Patrick's Day songs
and sing them to the tune of "Five Fat Turkeys" on page 57.

FIVE LITTLE PUMPKINS

Five little pumpkins (Hold up five fingers.)
Sitting on a gate, (Place other hand horizontally below
  the five fingers.)

The first one said, (Wiggle thumb.)
"Oh, my, it's getting late!" (Put hands on cheeks and shake
  head.)

The second one said, (Wiggle index finger.)
"There are witches in the air." (Move hand in wavelike motion.)
The third one said, (Wiggle middle finger.)
"But I don't care." (Raise hands with palms up.)
The fourth one said, (Wiggle ring finger.)
"Let's run and run and run." (Make running motion with
  fingers.)

The fifth one said, (Wiggle little finger.)
"I'm ready for some fun." (Clap three times.)
Oooohh went the wind and (Make wind sound.)
Out went the lights, (Clap hands.)
And the five little pumpkins (Hold up five fingers.)
Rolled out of sight. (Rotate hands over each other and
  hide hands behind back.)

FIVE LITTLE LEPRECHAUNS

Five little leprechauns (Hold up five fingers.)
Sitting 'neath a tree, (Cup other hand loosely over
  five fingers.)

The first one said, (Wiggle thumb.)
"Jump up and follow me." (Jump up once.)
The second one said, (Wiggle index finger.)
"But it's starting to pour." (Wiggle fingers and
  move hands down.)

The third one said, (Wiggle middle finger.)
"Look! Here's a secret door!" (Draw rectangle in air.)
The fourth one said, (Wiggle ring finger.)
"It's a perfect place to hide." (Cover eyes with hands.)
The fifth one said, (Wiggle little finger.)
"I can't wait to get inside." (Shake head and hug self with arms.)
Oooohh went the wind and (Make wind sound.)
Slam went the door, (Clap hands.)
And the five little leprechauns (Hold up five fingers.)
Were seen no more! (Hide hand behind back.)

WE WISH YOU A MERRY CHRISTMAS AND VARIATIONS

Christmas Song / Movement Activity

Steps:

1. At holiday time, teach your class the chorus of this traditional song:

   We wish you a merry Christmas,
   We wish you a merry Christmas,
   We wish you a merry Christmas,
   And a happy new year.

2. Ask children to stand in a circle. Have children sing additional movement verses, doing the actions in time to the beat. For example:

   Let's all do a little jumping,   (repeat two times)
   And bring Christmas cheer.

   Sing other verses, having children clap, hop, skip, tap, run, glide, and so on.

Variations:

1. Use rhythm instruments when singing this song. Select a few children to play tambourines, bells, rhythm sticks, drums, and so on, to the beat of the music as the other children do the actions. After each verse, the children with instruments will pass them to other children and do the actions while the others play the instruments.

2. For a movement activity at any time of the year, have children sing:

   We wish you a happy Monday,   (or whatever day it is)
   We wish you a happy Monday,
   We wish you a happy Monday,
   Each week of the year.

   Let's all do a little hopping,   (repeat two times)
   This time of the year.

3. Older children may sing this song as a round. Divide the class into two groups, and have the second group begin the song when the first group has finished singing the second line.

THE ANGEL BAND
Christmas Song / Rhythm Activity

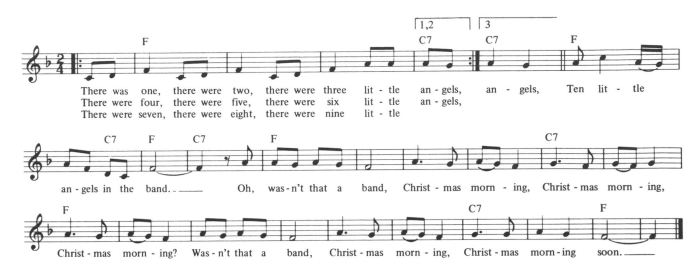

There was one, there were two, there were three lit-tle an-gels, an-gels, Ten lit-tle
There were four, there were five, there were six lit-tle an-gels,
There were seven, there were eight, there were nine lit-tle

an-gels in the band. ____ Oh, was-n't that a band, Christ-mas morn-ing, Christ-mas morn-ing,

Christ-mas morn-ing? Was-n't that a band, Christ-mas morn-ing, Christ-mas morn-ing soon. ____

You need: 11 assorted rhythm instruments: drums, bells, maracas, tambourines, rhythm sticks

Optional: 10 lengths of silver or gold Christmas garlands taped into circles to make "halos" for children

Steps:

1. Ask the class to sit in a large circle. Teach children this song.

2. Choose a rhythm instrument for yourself, and then pass out ten instruments to ten children. If desired, give these ten children halos to wear, made from silver or gold Christmas garlands.

3. Play your instrument and march around the outside of the circle as you begin the song. Each time you say a number in the song, tap a child holding an instrument to signal the child to follow you and play his or her instrument. Continue marching around the circle until the song is over.

4. At the end of the song, ask the ten children with instruments to give them (and the halos) to children in the circle who haven't yet had a turn.

Variations:

1. This song may be sung at any time of the year by substituting the word *children* for *angels* and the phrase *morning, noon,* or *night* for *Christmas morning.*

2. Create different holiday versions of this song. For example:

   Ten little goblins . . . Halloween morning.

   Ten little Pilgrims (Indians or turkeys) . . . Thanksgiving morning.

   Ten little leprechauns . . . St. Patrick's morning.

   Ten little bunnies . . . Easter morning.

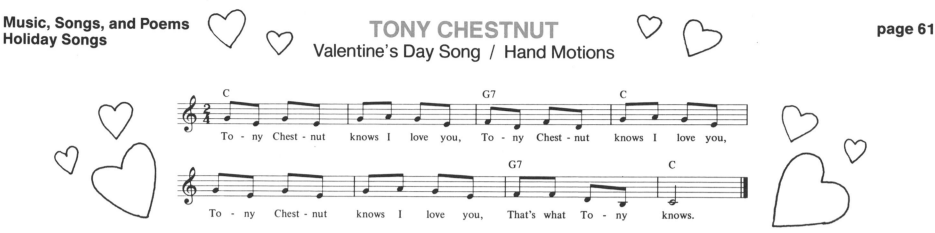

To - ny Chest - nut knows I love you, To - ny Chest - nut knows I love you,

To - ny Chest - nut knows I love you, That's what To - ny knows.

Steps:

1. Ask children to stand in a large circle.

2. Teach them the song and the actions shown below.

3. Tell children you are going to play a game with them. Ask them to sing with you and do what you do. Remind them to listen and pay close attention to what you do. Then repeat the song, changing the tempo from verse to verse. For example: Sing the song very slowly the first time and very quickly the second time. The third time, pause after the word *knee* and see if children wait until you continue the song. If a child does not pause when you do, he or she is out of the game. This is a useful listening and watching activity that can help get the attention of a class that has become too noisy.

To- (Child points to toes.)   *ny* (Child points to knees.)   *Chest-* (Child points to chest.)   *nut* (Child points to head.)

knows (Child points to nose.)   *I* (Child points to self.)   *love* (Child crosses arms in front of chest.)   *you,* (Child points to another child.)

HOP OVER, BUNNY

Easter Song / Bunny-Ears Headband

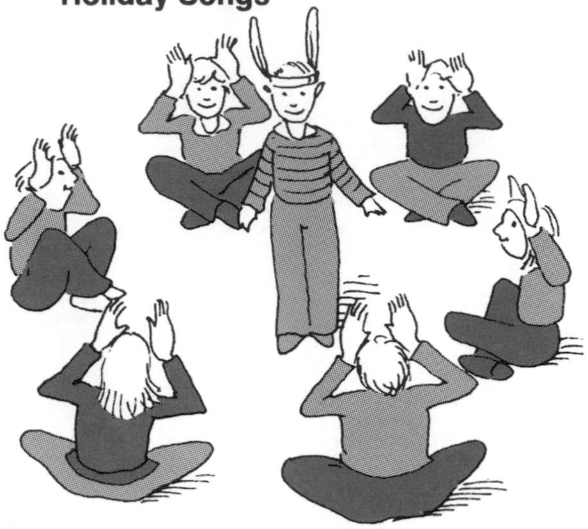

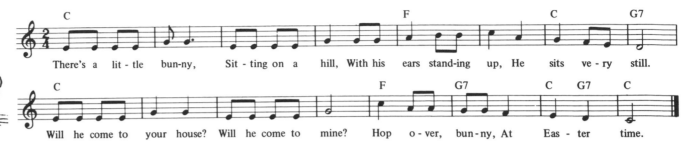

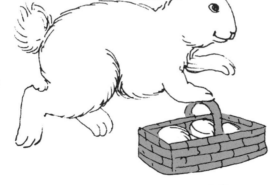

There's a little bunny,
Sitting on a hill,
With his ears standing up,
He sits very still.
Will he come to your house?
Will he come to mine?
Hop over, bunny,
At Easter time.

Steps:

1. Have children sit in a circle. Teach them this song.
2. Choose one child to stand in the middle of the circle as the bunny, and give him or her a bunny-ears headband to wear (see instructions on this page).
3. Sing the song. All children should hold their hands above their ears to represent bunny ears.
4. When the class sings "Hop over, bunny, at Easter time," the bunny hops over to another child in the circle and gives that child the bunny-ears headband to wear. That child becomes the next bunny to stand in the middle of the circle, while the former bunny takes his or her place in the circle.

BUNNY-EARS HEADBAND

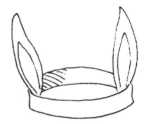

You need: ruler
pencil
scissors
18″ × 24″ white construction paper
stapler
9″ × 12″ pink construction paper
glue

Steps:

1. Measure and cut out a 2″ × 24″ strip of white construction paper.
2. Staple the ends of the strip together to form a child-sized headband.
3. Draw and cut out two white ovals, about 9″ high and 3½″ wide.
4. Next, cut out two slightly smaller pink ovals and glue each one onto a white oval to make bunny ears.
5. Staple the ears onto either side of the headband.

MICHAEL FINNEGAN
St. Patrick's Day Song

There was an old man named Michael Fin-ne-gan, He had whis-kers on his chin-ne-gan,

They fell out and then grew in a-gain, Poor old Mi-chael Fin-ne-gan, be-gin a-gain.

Verse 2

*There was an old man named Michael Finnegan,
He went fishing with a pinnegan.
He caught a fish, then threw him in again,
Poor old Michael Finnegan, begin again!*

Verse 3

*There was an old man named Michael Finnegan,
He climbed a tree and scraped his shinnegan.
He took off many years of skinnegan,
Poor old Michael Finnegan, begin again!*

Verse 4

*There was an old man named Michael Finnegan,
He grew fat and then grew thinnegan.
He slept and then got up to begin again,
Poor old Michael Finnegan, THE END AGAIN!*

You need: worksheet on page 64
crayons

Steps:

1. Teach this silly song to your class around St. Patrick's Day. Teach one verse at a time.

2. After the children have learned the song, increase the tempo of each verse. (Do not pause at the end of each verse, but continue directly into the next verse.)

3. When children are familiar with the song, make a copy of the worksheet on page 64 for each child.

4. Give each child a worksheet and some crayons. Then read the instructions on this page to the class as children complete their worksheets.

Instructions to the children:

Look at the picture of Michael Finnegan.
Color his hair red.
Something is missing on Michael Finnegan. It grew out and then grew in again. Do you remember what it was? (Whiskers.)
Draw what is missing on Michael Finnegan.
Michael Finnegan is sitting next to a big, blue pond. Please draw the pond.
Next, draw five fish in the pond.
Michael Finnegan loved to fish. But he fished with something very strange. Do you remember what it was? (A pinnegan.) Now draw a fishing pole in Michael's hands, with a pin at the end of the fishing line.
Did Michael catch any fish? (Yes.) Please draw a fish at the end of Michael's fishing line.
What did Michael do with the fish he caught? (He threw him in again.) No wonder he was thinnegan! Now color the rest of the picture.

Name _____